More of Him

of Him

Less of Me

What Does GOD Want?

Mark Krenning

First Printing

The Holy Bible, New International Version

Copyright 1973, 1978, 1984 by International Bible Society Used by Permission.

Hardcover 978-1-312-04612-2

PUBLISHED BY REVIVAL WAVES OF GLORY BOOKS & PUBLISHING

www.revivalwavesofglory.com

Litchfield, IL

Printed in the United States of America

Table of Contents

INTRODUCTION 5

The Re-Birth: A New Beginning 8

THE STRUGGLE BETWEEN flesh AND SPIRIT 18

The Prophetic and the flesh 31

Closing thoughts 40

2 Peter 1:3-11 "His divine power has given us everything we need for life and godliness through our knowledge of him who called us by his own glory and goodness. Through these he has given us his very great and precious promises, so that through them you may participate in the divine nature and escape the corruption in the world caused by evil desires. For this very reason, make every effort to add to your faith goodness; and to goodness, knowledge; and to knowledge, self-control: and to self-control, perseverance; and to perseverance, godliness; and to godliness, brotherly kindness; and to brotherly kindness, love. For if you possess these qualities in increasing measure, they will keep you from being ineffective and unproductive in your knowledge of our Lord Jesus Christ. But if anyone does not have them, he is nearsighted and blind, and has forgotten that he has been cleansed from his past sins. Therefore, my brothers, be all the more eager to make your calling and election sure. For if you do these things, you will never fall, and you will receive a rich welcome into the eternal kingdom of our Lord and Savior Jesus Christ."

INTRODUCTION

More of HIM.....less of me is about the process God has taken me through in order that I may be one with HIM and truly worship him in spirit and truth. Understand I am not there yet, I am still going through this process. As far as I can tell this process will not end until I pass or Jesus comes back. However, I now have the Key (weapons, knowledge) necessary to keep this door of God's KINGDOM open because of what God has allowed me to go through.

Most Christians don't understand nor do they want to hear that there is NO GOOD THING WITHIN THEM! I know I didn't. Especially with churches ignoring this every important process that must take place in every true believer. What I mean by this is that our flesh must be crucified. The church has watered down the word of GOD in order to build their own kingdom and not the KINGDOM of GOD. Many churches teach that all you need is salvation and everything will be fine I have an issue with this mentality mainly because the bible teaches that salvation is a new beginning or a re-birth. If you have been given this book by someone or someone has recommended it to you thank GOD for that person, because they desire for you to get a better understanding of GOD and how HE works.

When something is birthed it is the beginning of a new life and in order for that life to thrive it must go through a process. For instance, when a child is born they are completely dependent on others. As the child matures and grows, the child must be disciplined in order to be taught right from wrong. If a child is not disciplined they will become very unruly and the lines of right and wrong become blurred. **Proverbs 22:6 "Train a child in the way he should go, and when he is old he will not turn from it."** When a parent disciplines a child in love that child has a choice to make. If the child accepts the discipline in love, the child will mature and

6

become a healthy adult. However, if the child decides to not accept the discipline in love and rebel, the child becomes more rebellious and angry, leading to a dysfunctional immature adult.

You see our walk with GOD works the same way. If a believer accepts God's discipline in love they grow into a mature Christian. However, if a believer rejects God's discipline the longer it takes to mature in the things of God, if they mature at all. Churches are full of dysfunctional Christians. One way to tell if you are an immature Christian is to look at your prayer life: who does most of the talking? Ouchhhhhh!!! This book is about the process God has used in my life to bring me closer to HIM. BY NO MEANS IS THIS PROCESS COMPLETE. It is only by HIS grace and mercy that this book is being written. This process needed to start on a firm foundation, the foundation of Christ. There had to be a new beginning, but how?

The Re-Birth: A New Beginning

In order to have a new beginning you must first accept Christ as your savior. This may seem elementary to most readers of this book but sometimes I wonder do Christians really understand this. What I mean is, is Christ spirit (Holy Spirit) ruling our souls or is he just in our heads? Is HE truly Lord of our lives or do we just give HIM lip service? The best example I can give is how I finally realized I was a sinner and needed a Savior and I made HIM LORD of my life. This took years for God to accomplish in me! I am so thankful for HIS grace and mercy in my life.

I was brought up in a Christian home and was taught Christians values. I went to a Lutheran school for a short time, one my dad had taught at. I attended church most Sundays. Yet, something was missing. I can remember going to church one Sunday as a youth around 13 years old, as I looked around, I saw the same people I saw for years doing the same thing. Nothing seemed to change, not the people or the service, it was the same every Sunday. It was so routine, it bored me. There has to be more than this, I thought. Something is missing, but what?

This continued for years and at about 16 I started to look for other ways to fill this void. At first I used sports to fill this void. I was pretty athletic as a child so I spent much of my time playing baseball and basketball growing up. However, I was also one of the shortest if not the shortest on the field or court. I never really understood why God had given me this ability but made me so short. Until years later, this gave me a determination I would later need in life.

When my passion for playing sports began to fade I started looking for something else to fill this void. So, I started experimenting with alcohol. It wasn't several months later I started using marijuana. These were some real bad choices. In my head I knew what was right but I liked how these drugs made me forget about this void in my life. I was happy no matter what was going on in my life as long as I was smoking dope and/or drinking or so I thought. This continued for years. It was due to these choices I had no confidence and it came across in everything I did. It had gotten so bad I was unable to complete college or get a real good paying job. You see the drugs and alcohol provided the feeling I was looking for but were not the way to do it. Jesus is the way and the Life. My point is Jesus was only in my head and not LORD OF MY LIFE. Yet GOD did not give up on me. HE had plans for me. However, HE was not going to override my will. I had to make the choice to make Jesus Lord of my life. But was I ever going to let HIM be LORD?

It wasn't until my mid 20's that these things began to lose their effectiveness in filling this void. So the next thing I turned to was marriage. I wanted to start a family. This will make me happy, this will fill the void. In my late 20's I was married with our first child. Eventually we would have 7 awesome children altogether. So now I had to take care of a family, with no confidence and very little money. Could I do this? It was during this time, I began to seek out God, but how could I find HIM? The only thing I knew was church. I didn't own a bible at the time. Besides during all those years of Lutheran school all I knew was it was something I memorized a few verses from, but had absolutely no meaning to me. I could not understand it. I did not have the Holy Spirit. So, the only thing I knew to do was to start going back to church. So as a family we sought out where to go. At first going back to church felt good. It was the right thing to do. However it wasn't long before we started jumping from church to church mostly because I just couldn't take the same routine every Sunday again.

Then we were introduced to a prophetic church in the late 1980's. Someone had spoken with my wife and told her about a prophetic church starting up in our area. What was that I thought? This sounds interesting. The very next Sunday we attended the church service.

Shortly thereafter, we were convinced this was our church. Finally, something different, something new, this will take care of this void.

We quickly embraced the prophetic. It was during this time along came another child our second son. Wow, am I blessed another child. Our family rarely missed a service, if ever. It was at this church, Victory Lighthouse Ministries, that I realized I needed a savior. This did not happen immediately. You see I knew of Jesus before, but I did not KNOW HIM as Savior.

I can remember sitting through many invitations to accept Jesus as Lord and Savior thinking to myself did I need to respond? However, the thought left quicker than it came. I thought because I knew of Jesus, I was good, I reasoned with myself. But then I really began to look at myself. Something needed to change but what was it? I did not realize it at the time but God was moving. HE was drawing me closer. HE wanted a relationship with me and the only way that was going to happen was I needed to realize I was a sinner and accept Jesus Christ as Savior.

Then it happened. The most intense internal struggle I had ever faced to this point in my life. The alter was opened to accept Jesus as Savior, I sat with my head down struggling with the fact I was being drawn to respond. I remember thinking what would people think? You don't need to go up there, you have been going to church for years. My heart was pounding. Almost to the point it felt as if it was going to jump out of my chest cavity. My hands were shaking and sweating. Something did not want me to respond.

You see if you are not aware that you need a savior why would you respond to an alter call to accept Christ? We are born into sin. Sin is what we know, whether we realize it or not. So how do we even know we need to be saved, saved from what? I am a good person, I don't kill, steal, I help people, I have a family, I have a job, I go to church, I know who Jesus is. Jesus is lord and savior. God loves me! After all, this is what I was taught. I have heard this so many times and heard so many stories so I must be saved. I was living in deception and was about to be freed from this!

After what seemed like hours, but was only seconds I got up to respond. I responded out of ignorance, because I did not know how to quiet this intense internal struggle within. Once up front, I was truly led to Christ with the evidence of speaking in tongues which occurred a few seconds later. The freedom I felt cannot be described with words, but I felt something I had never felt before, a peace beyond words. The internal struggle that was so intense before was now replaced with such a peace I broke down and cried, but for only a few seconds because I didn't want anyone seeing this, after all I was a man I'm not to show this type of emotion.

What just happened I thought? This was so real, I knew something had changed within me but I truly did not understand, especially with my natural mind. I tried to share with others I knew outside of church, but all I got were blank stares. How do you share something that words cannot express and the natural mind cannot understand?

It is the Holy Spirit that draws one to Christ. We cannot lead someone to Christ through our own understanding. We can share what Christ has done for us. In other words present our testimony to how our lives have changed to others, but the work of drawing and opening up one's spirit is not accomplished through head knowledge. Head knowledge will not redeem your spirit.

This first prophetic word I ever received spoke about how my natural mind was in the way. Talk about confusing, this really caused me to get frustrated with my walk with God. But something in me knew this was right.

The bible teaches that we are to repent and we are taught we need to repent. However, what we are not taught is what does repent mean. It actually means that we need to change the way we think. In other words, think differently. We are to have the mind of Christ.

The bible teaches that Jesus only did what he saw the father doing. We are to renew our minds by reading the word so we can understand the things of GOD. Without the Holy Spirit it is impossible to truly understand the bible, let alone understand how God does things. The only way you can receive the Holy Spirit is through accepting Christ as your savior, not by attending church and acting like you have the spirit by falling down when someone prayers for you, which I was guilty of at first.

Finally, after all those years of God preparing me for that moment, I decided to accept Jesus as MY SAVIOR. No longer was he only someone I had head knowledge of, HE WAS MY SAVIOR and HIS SPIRIT was within me. The foundation was finally laid in my life. I now had the first key to the KINGDOM OF GOD-Salvation.

Without salvation it is impossible to know GOD. However, the bible describes this as a re-birth, a new beginning. Did you catch that? It is a beginning. In other words, now you can begin to understand GOD and

HIS ways and salvation opens up that door. Now I can boldly go before HIM and make my requests known. Little did I know though, what was a head of me? Would I allow HIM to be LORD.

THE STRUGGLE BETWEEN flesh AND SPIRIT

I thought the internal struggle for salvation was difficult, it only lasted several seconds. The struggle between flesh and Spirit was and is an infinitely more intense and narrow path. This was a battle I was totally unaware of and only now am beginning to understand. I was taught that salvation was the ultimate destination. I thought I had completed the race, now GOD could use me. I knew nothing about the flesh.

The struggle between flesh and spirit is for the control of your mind. You see what a man thinks he is. If your flesh is in control you are a soulish Christian. You are controlled by your circumstances, emotions, others, and your own worldly desires. This is a dangerous place to reside. But it is where the majority of Christians stay.

We must understand that the only power that Satan has is what we allow him to have. The only way he even has access is through our flesh. It is in our flesh that sin resides. Before salvation our spirit was not truly functioning, it only responds to GOD, who is SPIRIT. The bible instructs Christians to take up our cross daily. **Luke 9:23 "Then he said to them all: "If anyone would come after me, he must deny himself and take up his cross daily and follow me."** This is referring to crucifying the flesh. In short when the flesh is crucified then the spirit is in control and the spirit will only do what he sees the father doing. The Holy Spirit is responsible for teaching, comforting, and guiding us. However, it is up to each individual to crucify their own flesh daily so that the Holy Spirit can work through us. What does this mean though? We are not to be controlled by our emotions, minds, circumstances, or others. We are to be of one mind, the mind of CHRIST. Who did only what he saw the father do!

What is it that keeps someone from maturing as a follower of Christ? In two words: OUR FLESH. You see our example is Jesus Christ. HE is the one we all are to follow. HE is the one that made a way! HE has given us the keys to God's Kingdom through his life, death, and resurrection. The first key we need is the key of salvation. This key allows us to have a relationship with our creator GOD the Father. The whole purpose of the key of SALVATION is to open that door to the relationship with the FATHER. HIS blood was shed for the remission of our sins. He died that we might have life and have it more abundantly. **John 10:10 "The thief comes only to steal and kill and destroy; I have come that they may have life, and have it to the full."** Sin separates one from GOD. Jesus in the ONLY WAY! Once someone has truly received Jesus as their Savior, get ready because it is only the beginning.

Once I received Jesus as my Savior little did I know or understand what was about to happen or what I would have to go through in order for God to become number 1 in my life. Again, I am not there yet, but I am closer. I now see how truly merciful GOD is. Earlier I explained about the emotional battle I went through before I walked up front to receive the first key to the Kingdom. Everything within me was pulling me towards not responding to this invitation, but I went anyway. It wasn't until the writing of this book did I understand that that was my first confrontation, but definitely not the last, with my flesh! You see God's spirit was calling me and my flesh wanted nothing to do with HIM. It was at this same time I received the HOLY SPIRIT and began speaking in tongues. This was the 2nd key to God's Kingdom I received, The Holy Spirit; the teacher and comforter. I was unaware that the stage was set and now it was time for the battle to begin between spirit and flesh.

I wish I could say I always made the right choice and was led by my spirit, I MOST DEFINITELY WAS

NOT! Little did I know how deceptive my flesh was or that I must take up my cross daily and crucify my flesh willingly. In the beginning of this book I wrote about repentance and that it actually means to change the way you think. In other words, change what influences what you do. As a follower of Christ we are to be lead by the spirit and not by our flesh (OUR OWN DESIRES/EMOTIONS). Those that lose their lives will find it. **Matthew 10:39 "Whoever finds his life will lose it, and whoever loses his life for my sake will find it."** This is not an easy process. But have faith GOD knows what he is doing. HE created you, and he will never leave or forsake you. Nor will HE give you anymore than what you can handle. This doesn't mean, it won't break you. The best way to explain this is to give you an example in my life. You see years ago, I told HIM do what you have to do in me so that I may fulfill the destiny you have given me. Little did I know what was about to take place.

I thought I was on the road to success. Everything was great, I was moving up at my job, my marriage was awesome, and not only was my family the envy of the church, I was an elder at the church we attended, and my wife was an anointed worshipper. The only thing missing or so I thought was money. Life was good and I believed only to be getting better, especially since I had word, after word, after word about receiving finances from GOD from the prophets that came to our church. They spoke about how I would mange millions for GOD. Then one particular prophet came through that spoke something entirely different. His word from GOD was that I would be like Job and I was to get Job 23:10 within my spirit "… He knows the way that I take; when he has tested me, I will come forth as gold." You see GOD was preparing me for what was about to happen, the test he was allowing me to go through. What was God wanting? I have given HIM everything, or so I thought. How deceptive and prideful the flesh is!

It was years later but all at once everything came crashing down. First, our church ended up closing its doors and then my job was gone, this all within a matter of several months. It wasn't but a few months later my marriage fell apart although we remained living together. Everything that was important to me gone within several months. At the time I did not realize this but my flesh began to rise up because it was not in control. Why was this happening? Who wants to serve a GOD that treats me like this! I did nothing to deserve this! I went to church 3, 4 times a week. I raised my kids in church. I even cleaned the church. I was on the finance committee, I was on the worship team, I was even an elder. I served GOD! YEAH RIGHT!

I wish I could say that was all that happened but it was not. Everything I tried failed. Every job I had paid minimum wage or was part-time at best. At one time I had 3 part-time jobs all paying minimum wage. Another time I drove 2.5 hours one way everyday 5 days a week, this lasted a year and half then I was downsized. After that job I worked 2 jobs, which meant I worked 7 days a week for 3 months trying to provide for a family of 9. It was during this time we had to short sell our home and had a car repossessed by the bank.

Although, my marriage was falling apart we had remained together because of finances. Then it was my birthday, several days before my wife made it very clear she was interested in someone else and does not see their relationship together ending. Even though the marriage was basically over this really hurt. I wish I could say I handled this in the right way, I did not. So in an attempt to find some comfort for my flesh....I needed someone or something.

I had taken this day off and planned to meet some people from work for some drinks at a local bar/restaurant when they got off. As I was reaching for the door to enter the bar I clearly heard the Holy Spirit speak, "Do not go in." However, my flesh wanted this and was in total control. In I went at 4:30pm. It wasn't until after closing did I come out, around 1am. I was like a dog returning to his feed on his vomit. You see this is the life God had redeemed me from many years before. That night I received a DUI after totaling out my car in a single car accident in a nearby neighborhood. The shame was almost unbearable! I had hit rock bottom face first!

It was only by GOD's grace that that was all that happened. It was during the DUI classes I was required to attend that I realized how much grace GOD had given me. I was broken! This was the beginning of something new, but what? Even though I was broken my flesh was still alive and well. It was here I realized I needed to break off the relationships I had with friends because I was not strong enough to overcome my flesh.

I struggled to get back into church. I went from church to church in the area looking, searching for something but couldn't find it. I cried to GOD! However, it wasn't long before a family I had worked for and went to church with before, came back across my path. God used them, especially the oldest son, now my best friend, to restore HOPE. If it was not for them being obedient to God I am not sure I would have made it through this part of my life. You see these people introduced me to two Ministries that God has used to bring HOPE and TRUTH back into my life. These ministries are Kim Clement Ministries and Revival Waves of Glory. Also, Gateway Family Church is another ministry that has helped during this process, especially Donna Carlisle and her prayers. Others who have prayed for me that I am aware of are Rowan, who has recently passed, and Mary Cadaret and Stephen and Carolyn Battles. I am so grateful for all the prayers that have gone up on my behalf.

Remember earlier I said I told God to do what he had to do in me so I could fulfill my destiny....HE DID! He accomplished it 2000 years ago with Christ's death on the cross. Through this process God has given me a greater understanding of what was accomplished at the cross through Christ death and resurrection. This is something I had asked for so it is an answer to prayer. This is another key HE has given me to HIS KINGDOM. This key I must use daily because now it is up to me to apply it. You see in **Roman 6:6 Paul states, "For we know that our old self was crucified with him so that the body of sin might be done away with, that we should no longer be slaves to sin-because anyone who has died has been freed from sin."** It is my responsibility to apply this truth to my life. You see I fell

27

back into sin and ignored the Holy Spirit because my old self jumped off the cross and I did not remind it, it had been crucified with Christ.

Sin separates us from GOD. It is impossible to be obedient to GOD when the flesh and not the spirit is in control. GOD is spirit, and we must worship HIM in spirit and truth. Obedience is easy when the spirit is in control. My burden is light and yolk is easy. For example, Adam and Eve were in paradise in the beginning, while in the Garden of Eden, they were constantly in HIS presence. However, along came the deceiver, who spoke to their flesh. Once his lie was accepted by Eve the rest was just a natural consequence of dis-obedience, which by the way is sin. They were separated from GOD. GOD even spoke to both Adam and Eve and warned them what would happen if they did not obey HIM.

The problem with many Christians is that once they accept salvation they are done. We think that is it, there is nothing left to do, except go out and save the world. Remember it is a new beginning, a rebirth into the spiritual world where GOD resides. We continue with the old life style reminding ourselves what a good person I am, I go to church, I help people, God loves me no matter what, I can't overcome so why try. God has given us all we need to overcome and live a victorious life over sin. We need to apply what we know, listen to the Holy Spirit, and actively bend our will towards God. Also, GOD does love all people, but that doesn't mean HE approves of what they are all doing!

God's ultimate goal with anyone is relationship. That was what Adam and Eve had before the fall. Through the Lord Jesus' life, death, and resurrection, God has demonstrated his desire to have that relationship with everyone. However, each one must decide for him/herself to pursue this relationship with HIM.

During Jesus life he demonstrated the KINGDOM of GOD. His death demonstrated not only HIS grace and mercy but also HIS hatred of sin. His resurrection demonstrated HIS victory over sin and the death it causes.   Many Christians want the power Christ displayed but are unwilling to purify their souls. This is available for anyone that truly accepts Jesus as Lord and Savior and desires a deeper relationship with God.

Many Christians believe sacrifice is what GOD is after. This is not true. Jesus was the ultimate sacrifice. Then what is he after? It is obedience. The bible states that obedience is better than sacrifice. Jesus demonstrated this with his life and his death. Even though he knew the intensity he was facing while praying in the garden, he was about to face an even greater physical pain on the cross however, he did not let his flesh rule over what God was doing. He prayed that if it were possible that this cup be taken from him. However, not my will be done but yours. What an example to follow. How many of us spend our prayer time letting God know we aren't happy with what is going on in our lives. When we should be asking, that HE do what needs to be done in us so that we can hear his voice clearly that we may be obedient to HIS WILL.

The Prophetic and the flesh

Have you ever heard that personal prophecies are conditional? I would hear this and then think, you are only saying that just in case you missed it. It wasn't until recently that I now understand what is meant by this. A personal prophecy is given as a promise to what GOD will do, if you are obedient to HIS Spirit. In other words, it is HIS spirit within us we must follow not our own minds or understanding, which is the flesh.

The reason I believed that the prophets were covering themselves by saying that personal prophecies were conditional was coming from my flesh. My flesh did not want anything to do with being obedient to God's Spirit. It wants to be in control. So I can do as I please and if it doesn't happen then the prophet missed it, it has nothing to with me. After all God loves me and HE is a big GOD. What a revelation this was when the Holy Spirit revealed this to me. Again, the natural mind (the flesh) was in the way!

This never occurred to me until I began crucifying my flesh. God has allowed me to be put in some pretty intense circumstances in my life. The only way that change is going to take place is if we follow HIS Spirit and not our flesh. So how do we do this? Daily I remind myself that my flesh was crucified with Christ and it will not control me. I look to HIM and thank HIM for what HE is doing for me. I am learning that my emotions are not truth, nor are they what I should follow. I have learned that emotions are real, but they are not my spirit. God created them but they are not to be controlled by the flesh. Our spirit is to control them! This doesn't mean that we should not have emotions, or not show emotion. What it means is that we need to ask what is causing me to feel this way? Examine yourself! Is it an outside influence, circumstances, something somebody did or said, or something I believe (my mind) or is it coming from within, deep down within from my spirit.

The best book I have read on this subject was written by Watchman NEE called The Spiritual Man. Reading this book more than once at different periods of my life has brought much revelation and understanding. However, this needed to be coupled with the experiences in my life to truly understand what the author was getting at.

I am thankful for what God has allowed in my life because I would not have gained an understating of this without these circumstances. God did not do this to me but HE allowed it. God is able to use all things to work together for good for those that love HIM. I believe that crucifying the flesh is a must for every Christian that is serious about their walk with GOD and wants to go deeper. You see your mind desires to know truth but it only receives truth from the spirit. It is God's word that is sharper than any two edged sword dividing what is spirit and what is flesh. God has designed our minds to be filters. In other words, the mind is to be used to filter out what is spirit and what is flesh and we are to judge it. In order to do this we must crucify the flesh daily, know that GOD is in control no matter what and HE knows what HE is doing! For what a man thinks he is….ARE YOU GOD's? Who is in control you or is GOD?

The flesh is very deceptive and prideful. If you are having trouble with sin in your life it is because of your flesh. If you are having problems understanding the bible it is because of your flesh. If you cannot seem to get deliverance it is because of your flesh. If your spiritual walk is not progressing it is because of your flesh. The bible teaches that everything we need as Christians was accomplished at the cross. Jesus even stated, "It is finished!" So the only thing we need to do is identify with Christ and crucify our flesh. It wants control, I cannot stress this enough. It is a stench to GOD! You can be doing everything you know to do for GOD, but if it is of your flesh it will mean nothing.

The fact that we are to take up our cross daily tells me that this is something we must face everyday while in this present world. Great men & women of GOD have fallen because they had forgotten to crucify their flesh. Even in the old testament before the cross was available there are examples of how much God hates the flesh: Moses a friend of God, whom spoke with God face to face was not allowed to enter the promise land because of his flesh. In Exodus 17:6 Moses was instructed to strike the rock and water would come forth to provide for the peoples thirst. Then in Numbers 20:8 -12 Moses was instructed to speak to the rock, however Moses again struck the rock as before and **God replies "Because you did not trust in me enough to honor me as holy in the sight of the Israelites, you will not bring this community into the land I give them."** Perhaps Moses was frustrated with the people's unbelief and struck the rock out of frustration. It was the flesh Moses was operating out of, whether it was because this was how he had done it before or whether his emotions got the best of him. To God this did not matter, it was a stench to HIM because the flesh was in control. This was partial obedience, which is the same as not being obedient.

Jesus talks about how we must drink of his blood and eat of his flesh. To the natural mind this sounds cannibalistic and makes absolutely no sense. Some believe this means to take communion. We are to take communion to remind us of what God accomplished through Jesus on the cross, but it is much more than that. I find it difficult to express exactly what Jesus was conveying using the English language. This would be a book in itself. But as simply as possible he is saying do as he has done and allow God to have total control. Put God's will above your own. In other word's we cannot pick and choose what we are to obey. The bible teaches that even if we are guilty of not following 1 part of the law we are guilty of not following it all.

This may seem like an impossible task to our flesh and it is! Remember however, it is easy to obey GOD when following the spirit, in the flesh it is impossible. The difficult part is crucifying the flesh. It is Jesus' flesh and blood that is a pleasing aroma to GOD, which carried HIS Spirit. While our flesh and blood is nothing but a stench to his nostrils, which is our own will, emotions, natural mind, etc.

Also, God's grace is sufficient. Don't let the enemy bring condemnation upon you when you fail to crucify your flesh. Remember who you are in Christ and nail that flesh to the cross, reminding it that it was crucified with Christ 2000 years ago. Then watch and see what GOD opens up to you. But you must be sincere and not walk all over God's grace and what was accomplished at the cross. Playing Russian roulette with God is a very dangerous game. Many believe that HIS mercy and grace are just a license to live how they want. Not so, it is for those that are sincere and truly want HIM to be their LORD!

God has made many great and precious promises in HIS word! If you study these out you will notice that many of these are for those that follow HIM. Some are based upon principles and it doesn't matter whether you are a believer or not, if you follow these you will receive the benefit. But the really great promises, the ones that will last for an eternity are for those that love HIM and all are based upon obedience.

How many times do we grow weary in doing well because we do not see HIS promises fulfilled in our lives? In doing well is referring to being obedient and confident in Christ! I gave you an example of this in my life earlier when I said, "Why would I want to serve a GOD that treats me like this." **(see page 24)** God was showing me how deceitful my flesh was, I wasn't seeing with my spirit. I definitely did not have the mind of Christ. I had my own mind and wanted GOD to line up with me. Not me with HIM. The lesson that needs to be learned is when we start to become weary the flesh needs to be crucified.

2 Peter 1:3-4 "His divine power has given us everything we need for life and godliness through our knowledge of him who called us by his own glory and goodness. Through these he has given us his very

great and precious promises, so that through them you may participate in the divine nature and escape the corruption in the world caused by evil desires.

As Christians we must understand that GOD is never the problem, only the solution. If something isn't right it is always us. GOD is not the one that needs to change. HE never changes and never will! We are the ones that need to be conformed to HIS image. HE is the potter, we are but the clay on the potter's wheel.

There is an excellent book that recently was released before this one, that talks about the difference between God's system and the world's system (man's). When I read this I realized, that man's system is always about control because it is not of God's spirit but the flesh. In other words, man system's are not about trusting GOD, they are about wanting control. The book is titled, "Who is Your Source, Heaven or Earth." That is a question we must ask ourselves as Christians, WHO IS OUR SOURCE?

Closing thoughts

I often sit and think why does GOD allow satan and the evil spirits to be around still. The battle has been won. What is HIS purpose for this? He causes nothing but harm, seeking to destroy lives and make a mockery of HIM. I always come back to HIS ways are not our ways and HIS thoughts are not our thoughts.

It gets back to HIS desire is to have a relationship with everyone. HE desires that none should perish. Satan is a pawn in God's hand. He is only around because it is not time yet. This whole book and my life are an example of how GOD used what satan planned for destruction to fulfill HIS plan for my life. Through these experiences, many of which I am still dealing with, HE has drawn me closer, opened up my eyes in the spirit, and given me a deeper experience and understanding into what was accomplished on the cross and HE made available to me so that I might live life and live it more abundantly.

God is in the process of restoring my life, although it isn't happening as fast I would like (the flesh again). HE has been working all this time preparing for the right time to release the blessings in my life that will be used to further HIS KINGDOM. As long as I keep my flesh on the cross, I will have all that GOD desires for me to have.

I do believe there is much more I have to learn. This is only another beginning and another floor has been added to the foundation that was laid many years ago, in receiving Christ as my Savior. How many keys and how many floors does GOD have for me, only HE knows. But I now believe that I am much stronger in my faith and I trust HIM more than I ever have in the past due to the experiences I have had and knowledge HE has given me through these experiences. The writing of this book is just an example. I am so thankful for all that HE has done, is doing, and will do in my life.

LORD, I ASK THAT YOU WOULD OPEN UP
THE HEARTS OF YOUR PEOPLE SO THAT THEY
MAY ACCEPT THE TRUTHS YOU HAVE PLACED
IN THIS BOOK. HELP US TO KNOW YOU MORE.
DO WHATEVER YOU NEED TO IN US TO
ACCOMPLISH THIS. GIVE US UNDERSTANDING.
ABOVE ALL I ASK THAT YOUR WILL BE DONE
ON EARTH AS IT IS IN HEAVEN.

www.ingramcontent.com/pod-product-compliance
Lightning Source LLC
Chambersburg PA
CBHW021828090426
42811CB00032B/2077/J